KT-571-698

Withdrawn from Stock
Dublin City Public Libraries

MEXICO

Cath Senker

The LAND and the PEOPLE

Leabharlanna Poiblí Chathair Baile Átha Cliath
Dublin City Public Libraries

WAYLAND
www.waylandbooks.co.uk

Published in paperback in 2017 by Wayland

Copyright © Hodder and Stoughton, 2017

All rights reserved

Editors: Nicola Edwards
Design: Dave Ball and Angela Ball at D&A
Cover design: D&A
Map artist: Stefan Chabluk

ISBN: 978 0 7502 9812 4
10 9 8 7 6 5 4 3 2 1

MIX
Paper from
responsible sources
FSC
www.fsc.org
FSC® C104740

Wayland, an imprint of
Hachette Children's Group
Part of Hodder and Stoughton
Carmelite House
50 Victoria Embankment
London EC4Y 0DZ

An Hachette UK Company
www.hachette.co.uk
www.hachettechildrens.co.uk

Printed in China

Picture acknowledgements: All images and graphic elements courtesy of
Shutterstock except p12 (both) Corbis; p13(both) Corbis; p15(t) Corbis; p16 (r)
Corbis; p17 Alamy; p21 (b) Alamy; p25 (l) Alamy; p26 (t) Alamy; p29 (r) Alamy;
p31(r) Corbis; p32(r) Alamy; p40 (both) Corbis; p42 (l) Corbis.

Every attempt has been made to clear copyright. Should there be any
inadvertent omission, please apply to the publisher for rectification.

The website addresses (URLs) included in this book were valid at the time of
going to press. However, it is possible that contents or addresses may have
changed since the publication of this book. No responsibility for any such
changes can be accepted by either the author or the Publisher.

CONTENTS

Mexico on the Map 4

A Brief History of Mexico 6

Land of Extremes 8

Go Wild! 10

In the Ring of Fire 12

A Booming Economy 14

Maquiladora Manufacturing 16

Feeding the People 18

On the Tourist Trail 20

The Capital: Mexico City 22

City Life 24

A Land that Time Forgot 26

In the Remote Rainforest 28

Climate Catastrophe 30

Growing up in Mexico 32

All the Fun of the Festivals 34

Music, Murals and Sport 36

Chillies and Chocolate 38

The Great Divide 40

Tackling the Problems? 42

Looking to the Future 44

Quiz 46

Glossary 47

Index 48

MEXICO ON THE MAP

Mexico is a place of contrasts. It's a developing country in North America, sandwiched between the USA, the richest country in the world, and the continent of South America, with its pockets of wealth amid poverty.

Landscapes

In Mexico you can discover miles of dusty desert, climb to the dizzy heights of volcanic mountain peaks, or be drenched with rain in the depths of tropical forests. Then there's the teeming mayhem of northern Mexico's sprawling cities contrasted with the remote rainforests of the south and east, where indigenous people eke out their living.

Tijauana

MEXICO HAS THE 11TH HIGHEST POPULATION IN THE WORLD.

Mexico fact file

Population: 121,736,809 (July 2015 est.)

Area: 1.9 million sq km

Capital city: Mexico City

Highest peak: Citlaltépetl (5,675m)

Main language: Spanish

Currency: Mexican peso

The Mexican people

In Mexico, you can meet an amazing array of people and hear more than 60 languages spoken. On many faces, you'll spot a mixture of European and indigenous features – two-thirds of the population are mestizo or of mixed descent. Around one-quarter are descended from the original inhabitants of Mexico before the European invasion.

Whistlestop Mexico

A few things to do on a trip to Mexico...

⤊ Have fun in Cancún
(see page 21).

⤊ Try tasty tortillas
(see page 38).

⤊ See spectacular Teotihuacán
(see page 20).

⤊ Listen to mariachi music
(see page 36).

Ciudad Juárez

U S A

Monterrey

M E X I C O

Cancún

« Mexico has land borders
with three countries, the
largest at 3,155km, with
the USA.

León

Guadalajara

Teotihuacán

Mexico City

Puebla

BELIZE

Acapulco

GUATEMALA

A BRIEF HISTORY OF MEXICO

Way back around 1200 BCE, when Europeans still lived in small villages, the Olmecs created the first great civilization of Mexico. They built large towns where they gathered to trade, and constructed amazing monuments. The giant stone heads they built (right), probably portraits of their rulers, still stand today in southeastern Mexico.

LANDING IN PARADISE

The Maya and Aztecs followed the Olmecs. Tenochtitlán was the capital city of the Aztecs, with beautiful white palaces and highly decorated temples on pyramids. These were the stunning sights that met Hernán Cortes and his Spanish soldiers when they landed in Mexico in 1519. The invaders couldn't believe they had discovered such a paradise. Using their superior weapons, they overcame the Aztecs within two years and seized their gold, jade, turquoise and ornaments for the glory of Spain.

>> These well-preserved Mayan ruins are a popular tourist attraction in Chiapas in southern Mexico.

☑ FORCED LABOUR

The sixteenth-century Spanish invaders forced the indigenous people to work on their crop plantations and down their mines. Conditions were terrible, and many died from ill-treatment and disease. Somehow, a few survived to continue their proud traditions and culture.

FROM THE FIFTEENTH CENTURY, SPAIN TOOK CONTROL OF MEXICO, PARTS OF THE CARIBBEAN AND MOST OF CENTRAL AND SOUTH AMERICA.

Struggle for freedom

Three centuries later, in 1821, the Mexican people finally won their independence from Spanish rule. But in the 1840s, the USA fought Mexico and won a huge chunk of its territory. After decades of rule by a dictator, the revolution of 1910–20 brought in a fairer government that gave land from wealthy landowners to landless peasants. From 1929, Mexico was led by the Institutional Revolutionary Party (PRI), but its rule was unpopular with some, and many indigenous people remained in poverty. In the 1990s, indigenous rebels rose up against the government, demanding equality. The PRI government was finally ousted in 2000.

PEMBROKE BRANCH TEL. 6689575

⌃ Emiliano Zapata led the 1910 revolution. People who took part in the rebellion of the 1990s named themselves after him.

LAND OF EXTREMES

In Mexico, you'll experience the baking hot desert of the north, the comfortable temperate climate of the Central Plateau – a raised, flat area – and the hot, damp tropical rainforests of the south.

⌄ The city of Guadalajara has a pleasant, dry and mild climate.

Mexico's peaks

If you fancy a climb, check out Mexico's mountain ranges – the Sierra Madre Oriental (to the east) and the Sierra Madre Occidental (to the west). Down south are volcanic mountains including Citlaltépetl, the country's highest peak. Watch out – many of Mexico's volcanoes are active!

>> Popocatépetl, Mexico's second-highest volcano

⌄ The Río Bravo is usually shallow and sometimes people can even walk across it.

THE RIO BRAVO (BRAVE RIVER) FORMS PART OF MEXICO'S NORTHERN BORDER WITH THE USA.

⌄ Acapulco has a comfortable climate and great beaches, so it's popular with tourists.

From forests to beaches

The southern half of Mexico is in the tropics and has rainforests. It's hot below 900m, but the higher you go, the cooler it becomes. Take your umbrella – this region receives lots of rain. To relax, visit the long, sandy beaches along the Gulf Coast, where you'll find the world-famous resorts of Acapulco and Cancún. The beaches are the best places to swim: Mexico has long coastlines but few rivers or natural lakes.

FOCUS ON

☑ WET AND DRY

Mexico has wet and dry seasons. Much of the country has a rainy season from June to mid-October. Tabasco, the wettest state, has more than 300mm of rain on average in September.

⌄ Deserts aren't always dry! Here, a thunderstorm hits the Sonoran Desert.

GO WILD!

If you love wildlife, you've come to the right place! Mexico is fifth in the world for its variety of different species. It's home to more than 26,000 kinds of plants and over 1,000 types of birds – a mix of North and South American species.

⌄ The tough caracara will take on a vulture twice its size.

MANY MEXICANS CALL THE CARACARA THEIR NATIONAL BIRD, BUT A GOLDEN EAGLE APPEARS ON THEIR FLAG

≪ Mountain lion

Desert dwellers

In the Sonoran Desert, you'll find yucca plants, with long, stiff pointed leaves, and spiky cacti. Jaguars, mountain lions and coyotes roam, hunting deer, snakes and rabbits. If you're lucky, you'll spot an armadillo with its extraordinary bony plates, foraging for insects in the early morning.

≫ Armadillo

≪ Jaguar

Marlin

☑ FISH BONANZA

The Gulf of California is rich in fish, including massive swordfish and marlin — so common in Los Cabos that it's called the Marlin Capital of the World. Tuna, sardines, shrimp and anchovies abound too, so the coast is fantastic for fishing.

Tall cacti and flowering yucca in the Sonoran Desert.

Rainforest riches

Mexico's rainforests are teeming with wildlife. Evergreen and deciduous trees, palms and mangroves fill the landscape. Brightly coloured parrots and toucans fly around the trees, monkeys leap from branch to branch, cougars prowl for deer, and anteaters scour the rainforest floor, snuffling out ants and termites. The air is filled with bird song.

Keel-billed toucan

Parrots

11

IN THE RING OF FIRE

Lava spews out of Mount Colima during the dramatic eruption of 2015.

Mexico is in the Pacific Ring of Fire, so its people are no strangers to the terror of volcanoes and earthquakes. The country has nine active volcanoes, and eruptions are frequent.

MOUNT PARICUTIN IS THE NEWEST VOLCANO IN THE WORLD – IT APPEARED IN A CORNFIELD IN 1943.

Colima on fire

In July 2015, Mexico experienced its biggest volcanic eruption in over a century. Colima, the 'Volcano of Fire', violently erupted, sending molten lava down the mountainside. A cloud of ash and rock fragments exploded upwards to 6km above the ground, dramatically darkening the sky. The ash fell to earth, leaving a covering of several centimetres. Around 800 people were forced to flee their homes to safety, some wearing masks as protection against the thick dust.

⌄ People fleeing the Colima eruption.

Quake disaster

Earthquakes have proved devastating in Mexico. In 1985, the worst earthquake in the country's history hit Mexico City (right), killing thousands of people, destroying buildings and leaving more than 100,000 people homeless.

FOCUS ON

☑ **PROTECTING PEOPLE**

It's impossible to stop earthquakes and volcanoes, but the government tries to reduce their harmful effects. In areas at risk, civil-protection programmes teach people how to cope. Emergency drills are held in public buildings and schools, and leaflets in local languages provide safety information. Some schools have been rebuilt to resist earthquakes better. After the 2003 earthquake in Colima, two major schools with three-storey buildings were demolished and rebuilt as safer single-storey buildings.

>> An emergency drill on the anniversary of the tragic 1985 Mexico City earthquake.

A BOOMING ECONOMY

Mexico has one of the fastest-growing economies in the world, and the second-largest economy in Latin America after Brazil. It's rich in oil, gas and mineral resources. The country has state-of-art manufacturing – making cars is Mexico's top industry and the USA is its biggest customer.

MEXICO IS THE WORLD'S EIGHTH BIGGEST CAR, TRUCK AND VEHICLE PARTS PRODUCER.

Stacks of silver

The country is also blessed with precious minerals. It's the world's largest producer of silver – expert silversmiths make beautiful jewellery, cups and candlesticks. Mexico also produces salt, zinc, lead, cadmium, copper and other minerals.

⌄ A beautiful silver spoon with a traditional design.

» The silver mining town, Guanajuato, close to one of the most productive silver mines in the world.

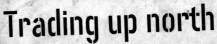

Trading up north

Since Mexico joined the North American Free Trade Agreement (NAFTA) in 1994, it's been easier to trade with the USA and Canada. The USA is Mexico's biggest trading partner. Much of its oil and more than two-thirds of its exports go to its large northern neighbour.

⌃ Many big-name car producers make vehicles in Mexico.

⌄ Mexico is the 11th biggest oil producer in the world.

FOCUS ON

☑ **CRISIS!**

Mexico was hit hard by the 2008 economic crisis, the worst since the Great Depression of the 1930s. But by 2010, the economy had recovered, and foreign companies invested billions of dollars in the country.

MAQUILADORA MANUFACTURING

M exico is unusual – it's the only important developing nation to be located right next to an industrial superpower. Foreign companies, mostly American, have found a clever way to exploit the situation: the maquiladora industries. They export parts to Mexico, manufacture goods there and import them home quickly and cheaply for sale.

MAQUILADORA INDUSTRIES ARE EXTREMELY PROFITABLE FOR US COMPANIES: WAGES IN MEXICO ARE JUST ONE-TENTH THAT OF US WAGES!

Growth

Some of the fastest-growing cities in Mexico have sprung up around the maquiladora industries; the population of Tijuana, just over the border from San Diego, USA, increased over 20 times from 1950 to 2005! It's now one of the biggest cities in the country.

Pros...

The maquiladoras are a mixed blessing. On the one hand, they provide plenty of jobs. There are also few natural resources in the dry, dusty desert of northern Mexico so these new industries are welcome.

《 Cramped shanty-town housing in Tijuana.

...and cons

On the other hand, the services in cities like Tijuana simply can't keep up with the numbers of people pouring in. Little rain falls, and there's not enough running water or waste disposal services for everyone. Many people have to buy water from the tankers that arrive every week. It's expensive and sometimes the water runs out. The maquiladora economy needs to become more sustainable.

⌃ In Salvador Urbina in Chiapas, people have to buy water for drinking and cooking.

⌃ Making clothes in a maquiladora factory in Tehuacán, in Puebla.

FOCUS ON

☑ GREY WATER

Some families in Tijuana have found a brilliant way to save water. They reuse 'grey water'. Water from showering, washing clothes and dishes is filtered through rocks to clean it and then used to water the garden.

FEEDING THE PEOPLE

The humble farming sector is nowhere near as important to the economy as it used to be. Yet it still employs one-fifth of the population, growing food to eat and cash crops to sell.

Major crops

Major crops are corn, sugarcane, sorghum (a grain that looks like corn) and wheat. Corn and wheat are staple (basic) foods. In central and southern Mexico, people make their tasty tortillas (flatbreads) from corn flour; in northern Mexico, they use wheat flour.

≪ Sorghum growing.

⌄ Mexicans cook corn every day.

Your five a day

As for fruit and vegetables, you're spoilt for choice. Local markets display delicious produce grown in Mexico. The temperate zones provide tomatoes, pumpkins and chillies, while sweet, juicy mangoes, papaya, pineapple and guava grow in the tropical areas.

A traditional market, selling locally grown fruit.

PEMBROKE BRANCH TEL. 6689575

FOCUS ON

☑ **HABITATS UNDER THREAT**

Mexicans are eating more and more meat, especially beef, and they're exporting it to the USA and other countries. Farmers clear large swathes of the rainforests to keep cattle. This is bad news for the wildlife. Monkeys, cougars and many birds are losing their habitats and are in danger of dying out.

THE OLMECS LEARNT TO CULTIVATE CACAO BEANS AND INVENTED CHOCOLATE. NEXT TIME YOU BITE INTO A CHOCOLATE BAR, THANK THE MEXICANS!

Coffee

Mexico is one of the world's major coffee exporters. The Chiapas region has the perfect conditions for growing coffee: good soil, cool weather, plenty of water and shade.

« Cacao beans grow in rainforest areas, especially Tabasco.

19

ON THE TOURIST TRAIL

Mexico has lots to offer tourists – spectacular Mayan ruins, elegant former colonial towns and beautiful coastlines. Tourism is a vital and growing part of the economy. Near Mexico City lies the ancient holy city of Teotihuacán. The biggest city in the western hemisphere before the fifteenth century, it has giant pyramids just as impressive as those in Ancient Egypt, all built by people's bare hands.

>> At Chichen Itza, near Cancún, you can marvel at a perfectly preserved Mayan pyramid.

European style

Visiting the colonial cities of Oaxaca, Puebla and Merida, you could be forgiven for thinking you were in Europe. In Merida, the Spanish invaders destroyed the ancient pyramids and used the ruins to build a cathedral and other European-style buildings.

<< The European-style cathedral in Merida – clearly different from traditional Mexican buildings.

MEXICO IS THE MOST VISITED COUNTRY IN THE AMERICAS AFTER THE USA: 29.1 MILLION PEOPLE VISITED IN 2014.

By the sea

Most tourists head to the beach resorts around Cancún in the Gulf of Mexico for sun, sand and sea. Once a quiet fishing village, Cancún has become a major tourist resort with soaring hotel blocks, shopping malls, casinos and golf courses. On the Pacific Coast, Acapulco is Mexico's biggest and best-known resort city, once the favourite haunt of Hollywood stars. But in recent years, it's been badly hit by violent crime.

FOCUS ON

✓ TOURISM PROS

Tourism brings jobs for local people in hotels and restaurants, and eager shoppers to buy hand-made souvenirs.

☒ TOURISM CONS

The workers don't get an equal share of the tourist dollars. Thousands of Mayans work in coastal tourism for low wages — most of the money goes to the big businesses that run the services. Many indigenous people have given up farming for these jobs, so they no longer grow their own food.

« Community tourism brings the benefits of tourism without the disadvantages: guides can earn a living showing tourists around traditional Mayan communities.

THE CAPITAL: MEXICO CITY

Mexico City is the centre of Mexico's government, business and media industries. The city sprawls for miles on a plateau so high that the temperature is a pleasant 15–20°C all year round. It's a bustling place full of traffic; the constant haze of car-exhaust fumes causes heavy pollution.

Old and new

The original Aztec city of Tenochtitlán was torn down by the Spanish invaders, who built Mexico City over the ruins in the European style. Now, it's a mixture of old and new buildings, with historic churches jostling alongside tall modern hotels. At the heart is a huge, noisy square, the Zócalo, while in the modern financial district, skyscrapers loom.

⌄ The skyscrapers of the financial district, with Torre Mayor (far right), one of the tallest buildings in Mexico.

MEXICO CITY HAS 21 MILLION PEOPLE – MORE THAN TWICE THE POPULATION OF LONDON

Suburbs and shanty towns

Most people live in the suburbs of Mexico City. In the west and south, the wealthiest people occupy mansions surrounded by luxurious gardens. Along the north-western and eastern edges are the ciudades perdidas – lost cities. Here, corrugated roofs and makeshift washing lines mark the shanty towns where migrants have hand-built their own rough shelters.

⌃ At the Zócalo, one of the world's largest squares, you might see dancers, concerts or protests.

FOCUS ON

☑ **CITY OF CULTURE**

Mexico City is one of Latin America's main cultural centres, with a mix of ancient and modern buildings and art, from pre-Hispanic ruins to colonial Spanish houses, nineteenth-century Mexican public buildings to cutting-edge modern architecture. Some say it has more museums than any other city in the world.

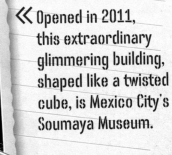

« Opened in 2011, this extraordinary glimmering building, shaped like a twisted cube, is Mexico City's Soumaya Museum.

CITY LIFE

No other Mexican city is anywhere near as large as the capital: the next biggest is Guadalajara, around a quarter of its size. Puebla, Ciudad Juárez, Tijuana, Monterrey and León are other important cities.

ABOUT 80 PER CENT OF THE MEXICAN POPULATION LIVE IN CITIES.

⌄ Hospicio Cabañas in Guadalajara was built in the early nineteenth century. This special building is now a World Heritage site and has international protection.

Guadalajara

Founded by the Spanish, Guadalajara has a historic centre full of old colonial buildings. Today it's a major industrial city and education hub, with no fewer than eight universities. It's also the base for many technology companies – Guadalajara is known as Mexico's Silicon Valley (after Silicon Valley in California, birthplace of the world's largest high-tech companies). And it's the home of traditional mariachi folk bands (see page 36).

Monterrey

Next biggest is Monterrey, partly surrounded by the Sierra Madre Oriental mountains. It's a hive of industry and trade, and has three universities. Monterrey is close to the border with the USA, so many migrants cross illegally from there. Owing to its location, it's one of Mexico's most Americanised cities, with huge shopping malls and neat housing estates. The city has been badly affected by drug violence but since 2014, the situation has been improving.

≫ A high-tech medical systems company in Monterrey.

FOCUS ON

✓ **SOMBREROS**

Some people believe that the sombrero – the traditional, broad-brimmed Mexican hat – was invented by horse riders from Guadalajara who needed to protect their heads from the fierce sun.

≫ Rodeo riders wearing traditional sombreros.

25

A LAND THAT TIME FORGOT

Around a fifth of Mexicans, many of them indigenous people, live on the land. Visiting remote farming areas is like entering a time warp – people live much as they did hundreds of years ago.

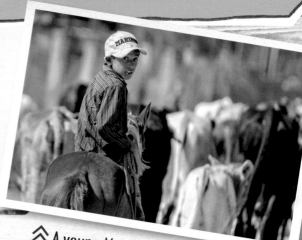
⌃ A young Mexican cowboy

⌄ These farmers are harvesting blue agave, used to make the drink tequila.

Labour on the land

Most work as labourers on farms, ploughing fields, sowing seeds or harvesting crops. Wages are low, so many are extremely poor. Others are lucky enough to own some land so at least they can enjoy all the rewards of their hard work. Farmers' children go to school in shifts so they can help their family on the farm the rest of the time – they're often highly skilled workers.

Crafts and clothing

Indigenous Mexicans are also excellent craftspeople, passing down traditional skills from generation to generation. They create clay pottery, embroidered cotton clothes, wool shawls, colourful baskets and rugs.

>> An indigenous woman makes a traditional huipil, a loose-fitting tunic.

SOME FARM WORKERS IN MEXICO EARN LESS THAN THE MINIMUM WAGE OF 70 PESOS (£2.80) A DAY.

FOCUS ON

✓ COFFEE FARMING

In the west of Chiapas, in the Sierra Madre Occidental, is a fertile coffee-growing area. The ripe coffee beans are picked, separated from their outer husks and then raked out to dry in the sun. It's tough work. Coffee beans are a cash crop, sold abroad to outlets where customers happily pay high prices for a latte or a cappuccino. But the farmers receive a fraction of the money for their beans. The people of Chiapas are among the poorest in Mexico.

>> A farmer dries coffee beans in the sun.

IN THE REMOTE RAINFOREST

Deep in the heart of the Lacondon rainforest in Chiapas live about 300 Lacandones (Lacondon people). The vegetation grows so densely that it is impossible to construct roads. People walk, or navigate the rivers in little wooden canoes.

Nature's gifts

The Lacandones still follow many traditional customs, surviving on the riches of the rainforest. They build their homes from wood, thatching palm leaves to build the roof; amazingly, a palm roof can last up to 15 years. A pipe brings in river water for washing, drinking and cooking. In a clearing, the Lacandones grow the corn, fruit and vegetables they need, following a pattern of planting that keeps the soil fertile. For meat, they hunt deer and other animals.

⩔ A wooden house with a palm-leaf roof
in the Lacondon rainforest.

Sustainable life

This is subsistence farming: growing just what you need and no more. Nothing in the forest is used up that can't be replaced, and nothing is ever wasted. It's a sustainable way of life.

Experts

The forest dwellers are plant experts – they know which are safe to eat and can spot the useful ones for making natural herbal remedies. They find plants to heal everything from painful wounds, cuts and scratches to poisonous snake bites.

« One of the Agua Azul waterfalls in Chiapas cascades through the forest.

⌃ A family in the Lacondon rainforest, with their lilltle pet monkey.

FOCUS ON

☑ RAINFOREST RAIDERS

Outsiders come to Chiapas for the rich resources of the rainforest but don't follow the Lacondones' careful ways. They cut down trees for timber and clear land for large-scale farming, destroying resources. This is called deforestation, and it's a huge problem.

MODERN LIFE HAS REACHED THE LACONDONES: THEY HAVE ELECTRICITY AND SATELLITE TV, AND THE CHILDREN ATTEND SPANISH-SPEAKING SCHOOLS.

CLIMATE CATASTROPHE

Few people live a sustainable life in the rainforests. Many farmers have adopted 'slash and burn' agriculture. They raze an area of trees to the ground, clearing space to grow corn or other crops. After a couple of years, the soil loses its fertility, so they move on and start again.

Deforestation disaster

Mexico has one of the highest deforestation rates in the world. Deforestation is not only damaging the rainforests but it's also causing environmental problems and even changing the climate.

>> Deforestation of the Lacondon rainforest continues at a fast and furious pace.

⌃ Southern Mexico now has more frequent and severe floods owing to climate change.

Rainfall

In forests, trees soak up water when it rains and their roots bind the soil together. On bare land, water runs straight off, causing mud slides. It flows into rivers, which rapidly fill up, burst their banks and flood.

Less rain

Rainforest dwellers have noticed that deforestation has reduced the amount of rainfall. Trees absorb more heat than bare soil. The heat warms the air, which carries moisture into the atmosphere, and it condenses (turns to liquid) as rain. Fewer trees mean less rain.

FOCUS ON

✓ GOING ORGANIC

Some Chiapas farmers have switched to organic coffee production. They grow their beans naturally without chemical fertilizers and plant trees to replace those they cut down. Organic farming is kinder to the environment and customers pay top prices for organic beans. With the extra income, farmers can invest in new equipment, such as coffee roasters to roast their own beans and earn even more money. This is sustainable development, creating a better quality of life for people now and in the future.

MEXICO LOSES ABOUT 330,000 HECTARES (815,000 ACRES) OF FOREST EVERY YEAR – A HECTARE IS ABOUT THE SIZE OF A SPORTS FIELD.

GROWING UP IN MEXICO

You might live in hectic Mexico City with all its sights and sounds, or in a sleepy rural village. But wherever you are in Mexico, all children go to school.

MORE THAN 9 OUT OF 10 MEXICANS OVER THE AGE OF 15 CAN READ AND WRITE.

School time

You start when you're six and are supposed to stay until 18, but if your family is poor, you'll probably have to leave earlier and start working. It's free to attend public schools. If your parents can afford it, they'll send you to one of the private schools, which are much better. The school day is normally from 8 a.m. to 2 p.m. but in rural areas, children often go to school in shifts – either in the morning or the afternoon.

El Pa
es tu

» Indigenous children studying hard at school near El Fuerte, Sinaloa, western Mexico.

« A boy sells souvenirs to tourists in Palenque, northern Chiapas.

FOCUS ON

✓ A TYPICAL SCHOOL DAY

You may start by singing the national anthem. There's a long morning of study — everything from maths, geography, Spanish, science, history and citizenship to sport. Around midday, it's break — you can run around outside, let off steam and perhaps play volleyball. Then it's back to the classroom to finish off your tasks and maybe get a head start on your homework.

⌃ Mexican children love their bikes!

⌄ Beach volleyball is hugely popular in Mexico.

Work and play

When school's out, you'll head home for a late lunch and to do your homework. If you live in the city you might have fun at after-school clubs, but in the countryside you'll normally help your parents, doing housework, tending the vegetable plot and feeding the farm animals. In your free time, you can play outdoors with your friends, ride your bike or join in a game of football.

ALL THE FUN OF THE FESTIVALS

Most Mexicans are Christians, so of course, they celebrate Christmas and Easter, but they have their own special festivals too.

>> A solemn religious procession on Good Friday

The Day of the Dead

It's 1 November, and the Day of the Dead fiesta is in full swing – Mexicans think the dead would be insulted by sadness. The streets around the cemeteries are decorated with flowers and brightly coloured paper art. A parade of scary-looking people, dressed up as skeletons and wearing skull masks, winds its way noisily into the cemetery. At the graves, people make a shrine to their loved one, placing offerings of food: pan de muertos (bread with bone shapes on it), candles, incense, marigolds, and most importantly, a photo of their relative. It's believed that the dead awaken to share the celebrations.

>> A Day of the Dead display in Mexico City celebrates the heroes of the Mexican Revolution and Independence.

>> Musicians playing in a cemetery on the Day of the Dead.

TRICK OR TREATING ON THE DAY OF THE DEAD HAS BECOME POPULAR, BUT THE FESTIVAL HAS NOTHING TO DO WITH HALLOWEEN.

‹‹ A traditional sugar skull

›› Decorations in the Mexican flag colours for Independence Day, Chiapas.

Mexican Independence Day

There's another big fiesta to celebrate independence on 16 September. The evening before, thousands gather in the Zócalo in Mexico City. The president rings a bell, a symbol of the struggle for independence from Spain, the crowd cheers, and fireworks light up the sky. In every town and city, Mexicans hang flags around the home and cook delicious foods in red, white and green, the colours of their flag.

FOCUS ON

✓ DAY OF THE VIRGIN OF GUADALUPE

On 12 December, Catholics celebrate Mary, the Virgin of Guadalupe, patron saint of Mexico. Catholics from around the country and further afield make a pilgrimage to see Mary's shrine in the Basilica of Guadalupe in Mexico City. Children dress in traditional costumes and thousands attend church.

35

MUSIC, MURALS AND SPORT

What are the highlights of Mexican culture? Mariachi music is a great favourite. You'll spot a mariachi group (right) on the streets at fiestas, often wearing elaborate silver-studded charro (cowboy) suits and sombreros. They'll be playing a cheerful folk tune on violins, guitars, basses, trumpets and the vihuela, a Mexican guitar.

Wall art

Around Mexico, you'll see huge murals – scenes from Mexican history and culture painted on walls. Artist Diego Rivera (1886–1957) and others made this art form popular. Today, many high walls in Mexico City are adorned with vibrant new street murals, often reflecting society's problems. The artists post images on social media networks so the world can view them.

« A faded historic bird mural in the ruins of Teotihuacán, Mexico City.

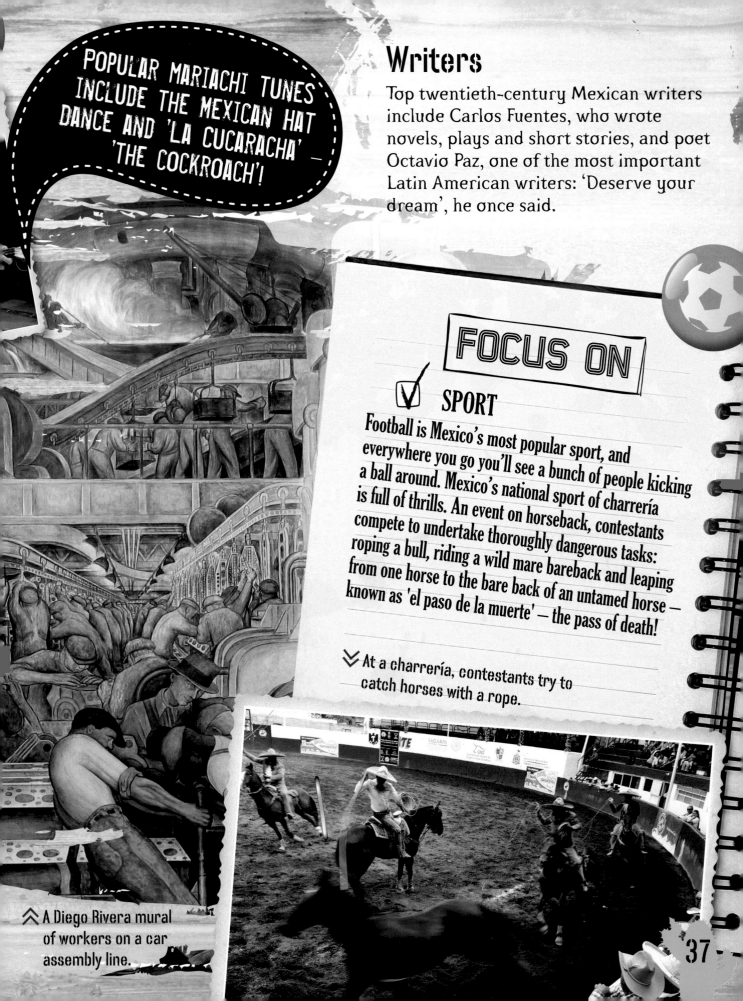

POPULAR MARIACHI TUNES INCLUDE THE MEXICAN HAT DANCE AND 'LA CUCARACHA' — 'THE COCKROACH'!

Writers

Top twentieth-century Mexican writers include Carlos Fuentes, who wrote novels, plays and short stories, and poet Octavio Paz, one of the most important Latin American writers: 'Deserve your dream', he once said.

FOCUS ON

☑ **SPORT**

Football is Mexico's most popular sport, and everywhere you go you'll see a bunch of people kicking a ball around. Mexico's national sport of charrería is full of thrills. An event on horseback, contestants compete to undertake thoroughly dangerous tasks: roping a bull, riding a wild mare bareback and leaping from one horse to the bare back of an untamed horse — known as 'el paso de la muerte' — the pass of death!

⌄⌄ At a charrería, contestants try to catch horses with a rope.

⌃⌃ A Diego Rivera mural of workers on a car assembly line.

CHILLIES AND CHOCOLATE

A major part of any country's culture is its food. With strong flavours and fiery hot chillies, traditional Mexican dishes are hearty and healthy to provide energy for working the land.

⌃ Huevos rancheros (ranch-style eggs), a traditional breakfast dish

Mexican mealtimes

Mexicans eat tortillas with practically every meal, using them to wrap food or to scoop it up. For a light lunch, you can munch an enchilada – a tortilla rolled around meat, beans or cheese. Dinner is the main meal – a pork, chicken or beef stew or perhaps eggs with refried beans and tortillas with avocado, cheese and vegetables. Did you know that Mexicans put chocolate in savoury dishes? For special occasions, you might have turkey with mole (say 'mo-lay') – a complicated sauce with about 20 ingredients including chocolate and lots of chillies.

MEXICAN HABANERO CHILLIES ARE SOME OF THE HOTTEST IN THE WORLD – EAT THEM IF YOU DARE!

« Chicken with mole sauce and side dishes

Junk food

The fast foods people adore in the USA have crossed the border to Mexico, and Mexicans love burgers, fries and soft drinks – one reason why a third of adults in Mexico are obese. The government is trying to tackle the issue: it has banned fried food and sweets from schools and brought in a tax to make fatty and sugary foods more expensive.

⌃ Making tortillas over a firewood stove

» Burger restaurants are very popular with Mexicans.

FOCUS ON

☑ **TYPICAL DISHES**

Burrito — wheat tortilla filled with meat and refried beans
Taco — fried tortilla folded in half, containing beans or meat, cheese and salsa (sauce)
Guacamole — sauce made with avocadoes, tomatoes, lemon juice and chillies

⌄ A variety of chillies

⌃ Chicken enchiladas, often eaten with guacamole

THE GREAT DIVIDE

Poverty, drugs, crime and illegal migration – Mexico certainly has its negative side. There's a huge gulf between the rich few and the poor majority scraping a living in the countryside and the shanty towns.

>> A Mexico City shanty town with shiny new buildings in the background, showing the gap between rich and poor.

Murderous drug wars

Mexico has a horrifying level of violent crime, with a murder rate about four times higher than the USA. Many gruesome killings are linked to the drug cartels. These cartels control the valuable drugs trade from South America to the USA. To boost their profits further, cartels kidnap wealthy people for ransom – Mexico has one of the highest rates of kidnapping in world.

<< An armed soldier taking part in the fight against the drug cartels in Ciudad Juarez, northern Mexico.

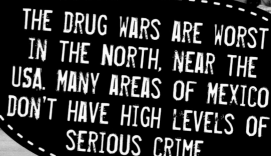

THE DRUG WARS ARE WORST IN THE NORTH, NEAR THE USA. MANY AREAS OF MEXICO DON'T HAVE HIGH LEVELS OF SERIOUS CRIME.

Cartels

There are thousands of rival cartels, which fight each other in deadly street battles. The police are supposed to stop them, but many officers are corrupt (see page 42) and are also working for the cartels.

FOCUS ON

☑ MEXICAN MIGRATION

Some desperately poor Mexicans try to cross the 3,000-km-long border to the USA, where work is more plentiful and wages higher. But the USA is strict about who it will allow in, so migrants may pay vast sums of money to people smugglers to sneak them over the border. Many are arrested and sent straight back. Since the 2008 economic downturn in the USA, fewer have risked the journey — the decline in jobs available means it's not worthwhile. And the Mexican economy has picked up, so there are more opportunities at home.

⌄ Agua Prieta, a city that reaches right to the US border fence.

⌃ A woman places a Mexican flag next to shoes belonging to victims of the drug war in Monterrey.

TACKLING THE PROBLEMS?

The Institutional Revolutionary Party (PRI) has dominated the country for the last century. It ran the country from 1929 to 2000 and returned to power in 2012 under President Enrique Peña Nieto. Can the government tackle Mexico's difficulties?

Corrupt to the core

Corruption is a major issue in Mexico – many people in power act dishonestly. The government may give money to a town for new buildings in return for votes for the ruling party. In poor areas, some politicians buy votes from people in return for supermarket gift cards. Nieto's government has promised to challenge corruption and tackle drug violence.

⌃ President Enrique Peña Nieto at a PRI event, 2015

MEXICO IS OFFICIALLY A DEMOCRACY AND IF YOU'RE OVER 18 YOU HAVE TO VOTE OR PAY A FINE.

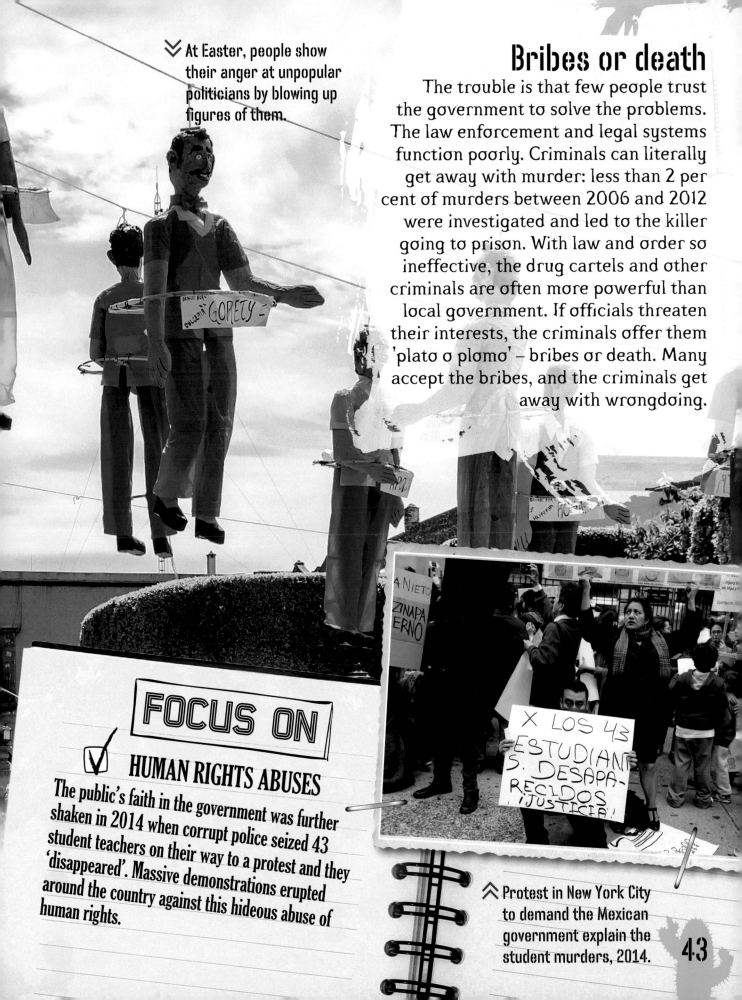

At Easter, people show their anger at unpopular politicians by blowing up figures of them.

Bribes or death

The trouble is that few people trust the government to solve the problems. The law enforcement and legal systems function poorly. Criminals can literally get away with murder: less than 2 per cent of murders between 2006 and 2012 were investigated and led to the killer going to prison. With law and order so ineffective, the drug cartels and other criminals are often more powerful than local government. If officials threaten their interests, the criminals offer them 'plato o plomo' – bribes or death. Many accept the bribes, and the criminals get away with wrongdoing.

FOCUS ON

☑ **HUMAN RIGHTS ABUSES**

The public's faith in the government was further shaken in 2014 when corrupt police seized 43 student teachers on their way to a protest and they 'disappeared'. Massive demonstrations erupted around the country against this hideous abuse of human rights.

Protest in New York City to demand the Mexican government explain the student murders, 2014.

43

LOOKING TO THE FUTURE

What is the way forward for Mexico? President Nieto's 2014 energy reforms allowed businesses to invest in government-owned energy companies and expand the production of oil and gas to fuel Mexico's economic growth.

⌃ In 2013, three-quarters of Mexico's energy came from thermal power (heat from burning fossil fuels).

Opposing energy reform

Critics of Nieto's energy reforms argued that they allow parts of the state-owned energy companies to be sold off to international companies, so the profits would no longer all flow to the government. And although the government is putting money into renewable energy, it is also investing in fracking to extract shale gas. Fracking is a controversial activity, as protestors argue that it can pollute the water supply.

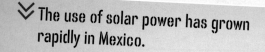

⌄ The use of solar power has grown rapidly in Mexico.

Natural issues

But what about reducing the huge gap between rich and poor? Unless this is addressed, there could be another uprising like the rebellion of the 1990s (see page 7). And what about Mexico's other social problems, its continuing drug wars, government corruption and human rights abuses?

Still, Mexico has lots going for it – plentiful natural resources, stunning historic sites, strong industries, a thriving farming sector and enterprising people. Perhaps in time these strengths will allow the Mexican people to overcome their country's problems and create a brighter future.

FOCUS ON

☑ **HOPEFUL SIGNS**

The government intends to pump money into renewable energies to make use of Mexico's plentiful wind and sunshine. In addition, new laws are being passed which aim to improve the justice system, promote open government and encourage people to become involved in politics.

⌄ The Teotihuacán Pyramids continue to attract huge numbers of tourists.

THE GOVERNMENT AIMS TO INCREASE ENERGY PRODUCTION FROM RENEWABLE SOURCES FROM 6 PER CENT IN 2013 TO 35 PER CENT BY 2025.

QUIZ

How much do you know about Mexico's land and people? Try this quick quiz and find out!

1) Which people invented chocolate?
a) The Spanish
b) The Maya
c) The Olmecs

2) When did Colima, the Volcano of Fire, last erupt?
a) 2015
b) 2014
c) 2005

3) What is a maquiladora?
a) A car factory
b) A factory run in Mexico by a foreign country
c) A Mexican drink

4) What's the normal school day in Mexico?
a) 8 a.m. to 3 p.m.
b) 8 a.m. to 2 p.m.
c) 9 a.m. to 2 p.m.

5) What's special about Mexican mole sauce?
a) It's made with lots of ingredients including chillies
b) It contains moles
c) It's always eaten with turkey

6) Which of these is a beach resort?
a) Citlaltépetl
b) Guadalajara
c) Cancún

7) What do Mexicans celebrate on 1 November?
a) Halloween
b) The Day of the Dead
c) Independence Day

8) Which of these is not an example of sustainable development?
a) Organic farming
b) Subsistence farming of the Lacondon people
c) Slash and burn agriculture

9) Where is the Río Bravo?
a) On the border with the USA
b) In the southern rainforest
c) Running through Mexico City

True or false?
1) More than 60 languages are spoken in Mexico.
2) Tabasco is the driest state in Mexico.
3) Guacamole is a sauce made with chocolate.

Answers: 1c, 2a, 3b, 4b, 5a, 6c, 7b, 8c, 9a True or false? 1T, 2F, 3F

GLOSSARY

civilization
A state of human society that is very developed and organized.

colonial
To do with a country that controls another country – Spain was the colonial power in Mexico for about 300 years.

corrupt
Describes people who are willing to use their power to do dishonest or illegal things in return for money or benefits

deforestation
Cutting down or burning the trees in an area.

dictator
A ruler who has complete power over a country.

'disappeared'
A person who has been taken away by the police and no one knows what has happened to him or her; often, the person has been killed.

drug cartel
A criminal organization that controls the illegal drug trade

fracking
Forcing liquid at high pressure into rocks to open cracks and take out oil or gas.

indigenous
Belonging to a particular place rather than coming to it from somewhere else.

mangrove
A tropical tree that grows in mud or at the edge of rivers and has roots above ground.

maquiladora
A factory in Mexico run by a foreign country.

mariachi
Traditional Mexican music.

mestizo
A Latin American with Spanish and indigenous ancestors.

migration
The movement of people from one place to another.

organic
Of farming, produced by natural methods and without man-made chemicals.

patron saint
A Christian saint who is believed to protect a particular place or group of people.

plateau
An area of flat land that is higher than the land around it.

pre-Hispanic
To do with the time before the Spanish arrived.

renewable energy
Energy is replaced naturally and can be used without the risk of finishing it all – such as energy from the wind and sun.

sustainable
Involving the use of natural products and energy in a way that does not harm the environment.

temperate
Having a mild temperature – it never becomes very hot or very cold.

tropical
To do with the tropics, the hottest part of the world.

Further information

Books
Unpacked: Mexico by Susie Brooks
(Wayland, 2015)

Food and Cooking Around the World: Mexico
by Rosemary Hankin
(Wayland, 2015)

Mexico by Sarah Tieck
(Big Buddy Books, 2013)

Let's Learn About Mexico
by Yuko Green
(Dover Children's, 2013)

Mexican Culture
by Lori McManus
(Heinemann, 2012)

Websites
www.bbc.co.uk/
programmes/p0114db0
BBC Primary Geography:
Mexico

www.nationalgeographic.
org/media/dia-de-los-
muertos/
Day of the Dead

www.natgeokids.com/
uk/discover/geography/
countries/country-fact-
file-mexico
National Geographic Kids
Country Fact File: Mexico!

Index

area 4
Aztecs 6, 22

beaches 9, 21
business 21, 22, 44

capital city (Mexico
    City) 4, 13, 20, 22, 23,
    24, 32, 35, 36
children 26, 29, 32, 35
chillies 18, 38, 39
chocolate 19, 38
Christians 34
cities 4, 16, 17, 20, 21, 24,
    25
    Ciudad Juárez 24
    Guadalajara 24, 25
    León 24
    Merida 20
    Monterrey 24, 25
    Oaxaca 20
    Puebla 20, 24
    Tijuana, 16, 17, 24
ciudades perdidas (lost
cities) 23
civil-protection
 programmes 13
climate change 30, 31
coastlines 9, 20
coffee 19, 27, 31
corruption 41, 42, 43, 45
Cortes, Hernán 6
crafts 27
crime 21, 40
crops 18, 26, 27, 30
culture 7, 23, 36, 38
currency 4

deforestation 29, 30, 31
democracy 42
desert 8, 10, 16
    Sonoran Desert 10

drug cartels 40, 41, 43
drug violence 25, 42, 45

earthquakes 12, 13
economic crisis 15, 41
economy 14, 15, 17, 18,
    20, 21
education 24
electricity 29
emergency drills 13
energy reforms 44
eruptions 12
exports 15, 19

farming 18, 19, 21, 26, 27,
    30, 31, 45
festivals 34, 35
    Day of the Dead 34, 35
fishing 11, 21
food 5, 18, 21, 35, 38, 39
forced labour 7
fracking 44
Fuentes, Carlos 37

gas 14, 44
government 7, 13, 22, 39,
    42, 43, 44, 45
'grey water' 17
Gulf Coast 9, 21

habitats 19
herbal remedies 29
highest peak
    (Citlaltépetl) 4, 8
human rights abuses 43,
    45

independence 7, 35
indigenous people 4, 7,
    21, 26, 27
industry 14, 25, 44, 45

kidnapping 40

Lacandones 28, 29
land borders 5, 9, 16, 25,
    39, 41

landowners 7, 26
languages 4, 13
legal system 43

maquiladora industries
    16, 17
mariachi music 5, 24, 36,
    37
markets 18
Maya 6
Mayans 20, 21
media 22
migrants 23, 25, 41
mineral resources 14
mountain ranges 8, 25, 27
murals 36

national anthem 33
national sport 37
North American Free
Trade Agreement
    (NAFTA) 15

obesity 39
oil 14, 15, 44
Olmecs 6, 19
organic farming 31

Pacific Ring of Fire 12
palaces 6
patron saint 35
Paz, Octavio 37
peasants 7
people smugglers 41
plants 10, 29
plateau 8, 22
pollution 22
population 4, 16, 18, 22,
    24
poverty 7, 27, 40, 41

rainforests 8, 9, 11, 19, 28,
    29, 30, 31
rainy season 9
renewable energies 44, 45
resorts 9, 21
Río Bravo 9

Rivera, Diego 36
ruins 20, 22, 23

school 13, 26, 29, 32, 33,
    39
services 17
Silicon Valley 24
silver 14
'slash-and-burn'
    agriculture 30
social media 36
sombreros 25, 36
Spain 6, 7, 23, 24, 29, 35
sport 33, 37
stone heads 6
suburbs 23
sustainable economy 17
sustainable living 28, 30,
    31

tax 39
technology 24
temples 6
Teotihuacán 5, 6, 20
tortillas 5, 18, 38, 39
tourists 20, 21
trade 6, 15, 25
traffic 22

universities 24, 25
USA 4, 5, 7, 9, 14, 15, 16,
    19, 21, 25, 39, 40, 41

volcanoes 8, 12, 13

waste disposal 17
water 17, 19, 28, 30, 44
wildlife 4, 10, 11, 19

Zapata, Emiliano 7
Zócalo 22, 35